Trends and Issues of Economics and Workforce Development:

Workforce Training & Development, Course Outline & Project

Dawn D. Boyer, Ph.D.

Book Copyright:	2017© by Dawn D. Boyer, Ph.D.
ISBN Numbers:	ISBN-13: 978-1-948149-06-8 ISBN-10: 1-948149-06-0
Copyright Notice:	The Author supports copyright. Copyright sparks creativity, encourages diverse viewpoints, and promotes free speech, and creates a vibrant and rich art culture. Thank you for buying an authorized copy of this copyrighted book and for complying with international copyright laws. All copyrights are reserved. No part of this book, including interior design, cover design, icons, and pictures, may be reproduced, or transmitted in any form, by any means (electronic, photocopying, recording, or otherwise) without the prior written permission of the copyright owner. Independent of the author's economic rights, and even after the transfer of the said rights, the author shall have the right to claim authorship of the work and to object to any distortion, modification of, and/or other derogatory action in relation to the said work that could be deemed prejudicial to the author's honor or reputation. No part of this book or images – black and white, or other renditions of images, are to be posted to any social media, Internet, and/or other digital media or platforms without prior written permission of the copyright owner. You are supporting writers and allowing the author to continue to publish books for every other reader to continue to enjoy.
Trademarks:	All brand names, product names, logos, service marks, trademarks or registered trademarks are trademarks of their respective owners.

Author's Business Website	www.DBoyerConsulting.com
Amazon Author Page:	https://www.amazon.com/author/dawnboyer
Review Author's Books:	www.shelfari.com/DawnDeniseBoyer
Facebook Author's Page:	www.facebook.com/DawnBoyerAuthor
Facebook Business Page:	www.Facebook.com/DBoyerConsulting
Google+ Business Page:	https://plus.google.com/112802498128568560150/about?hl=en
LinkedIn	www.linkedin.com/in/DawnBoyer
Twitter:	www.Twitter.com/Dawn_Boyer

INTRODUCTION

Between 2009 and 2012 the author completed coursework for a Doctorate of Philosophy in Occupational and Technical Studies (STEMPS), with a concentration on Training and Development in Human Resources. The Ph.D. coursework and research was conducted and completed at Old Dominion University, Norfolk, VA.

One of the mandatory program courses was Trends and Issues of Economics and Workforce Development and was completed in the Fall of 2010. The course required completion of several segments of research, analysis, interviews, surveys, and application of findings to a report that provided suggested curriculum development and workforce training based on the findings and literature reviews.

This book provides the student's examples of coursework completed per the mandated project work, and conclusions based on the research and analysis work during this class. The book can be used as a model guideline to completing similar project in this class for future students, or as a baseline model upon which to complete workforce development research focused within a specific geographic area.

TRENDS & ISSUES OF ECONOMICS & WORKFORCE

COURSE DESCRIPTION

An analysis of economic trends & issues that lead to workforce development decisions.

Focus is on planning for educational & training programs to meet workforce needs dictated by local & regional economic issues.

This course is designed for community college & school system personnel.

Purpose

The major purpose of Old Dominion University's education program is to prepare individuals with in-depth knowledge of their chosen discipline and who can plan and present state-of-the-art instruction to students of various cultural and socioeconomic backgrounds and attitudes. The educator students should also reflect commitment to teaching and learning, as well as lifelong professional growth and development.

The Conceptual Framework, *Educator as Professional*, reflects the development of professional educators who can use their skills as pedagogical and academic teachers and educations, with their abilities to educate all students. This STEMPS department course was designed to aid professional educators in understanding the issues relating workforce education to the economic development of communities and regions.

Economic indicators can provide direction to focused needs for workforce education to a geographic or socio-economic target market. This course will study these factors that lend themselves to assisting community college, career-, technical-education administrators, and faculty to plan, with partners in business, industry, and government, to develop educational and workforce training programs that meet the needs of both the students and the geographic community.

Required Course Outcomes

Economic Indicators

Select an economic indicator and prepare a graphic presentation with supporting handout on one major economic indicator, e.g., construction, durable goods, heavy equipment, or investment.

Regional Development:

Present a report, using employment databases, that shows a need for workforce training and development for a geographic region. Respond and reflect to the estimates reported from the selected databases.

Employer Survey:

Contact three 'large employers' from your geographic region. Collect data from those representatives regarding their company's employee training needs. The report should include questions asked of them to solicit responses for their company's training needs, the data collected, and its analytical summary, as well as a description and outline of programs proposed to meet the employers' needs.

Strategic Plan:

Develop a plan with goals, strategic objectives, and training timelines for the proposed workforce education for the community or region.

Professional Development:

Outline a one-year professional development program for co-workers to increase awareness of local employers and plans for partnerships with those employers.

Return on Investment (Doctoral Students):

Present a plan for calculating the Return on Investment (ROI) for a work unit or department in which the learner is personally involved.

Course Competencies

This course is designed to assist professional, career educators in understanding issues relating to workforce education and connected to the economic development of communities and regions.

Competencies 1 & 2

The learner will explain major economic indicators that contribute to development of nations, regions, and communities.
The learner will identify state and federal legislative acts that guide education initiatives related to economic and workforce development.

Competencies 3 & 4

The learner will describe federal and state databases that provide data on job training needs for states and regions.

The learner will conduct a need's assessment for workforce training and program development with regional business, industry, and government facilities.

Competencies 5 & 6

The learner will be able to explain and describe workforce initiatives such as Tech Prep, High Schools That Work, School to Work Transition, Advanced Technology Centers, etc.

The learner will identify and describe articulated educational efforts between high schools, community colleges, and universities.

Competencies 7 & 8

The learner will be able to use strategic planning to close the gap between economic development and workforce education.

The learner will plan professional development programs for faculty to attempt to increase local education system's faculties' awareness of local business, industry, and government and plan educational partnerships.

Requirement A

The learner will select an economic indicator and prepare a graphic presentation with a supporting presentation on a major economic indicators, e.g., construction, durable goods, heavy equipment, and/or investment.

Requirement B

The learner will present using employment databases showing the need for workforce training and development for a specific region with a response and recommendations to estimates and suggestions reported from the selected databases.

Requirement C

The learner will contact three large employers from their economic region and collect data from those employer's companies regarding their employee training needs. The report should include questions asked to solicit data about the training needs, data collected, a summary, and a description and outline of programs proposed to meet the employer's needs.

Requirement D

The learner will develop a strategic plan with goals, objectives, and timelines for workforce education for a specific community or region.

Requirement E

The learner will outline a one-year professional development program for co-workers that will increase awareness of local employers and plan for symbiotic partnerships.

Requirement F

Doctoral Students.

The learner will present a plan for calculating the Return on Investment (ROI) for the work unit or department in which they work.

PROJECT FOCUS

The focus was on an area of the state of Virginia, southwest of Richmond, because there was a possibility of the researcher moving into this geographic area with a focus retirement in the next 10 years. The reason that area is of interest is there are two higher institutions of learning (Longwood University & Hampton-Sydney College) as well as two community colleges within commuting distance from the town of Farmville. The presence of the schools indicated potential for the Ph.D. to be employed by the institutions in the near future.

This geographic research baseline provided a place to potentially work within the training and development or educational field (STEMPS). The alternative would be to live within a locality with potential employment based on the student's background and experience for the human resources field. The question should answer: what will this area of the state need in workforce development in the future (based on the current statistics and metrics related to the population, the educational venues, the economic growth).

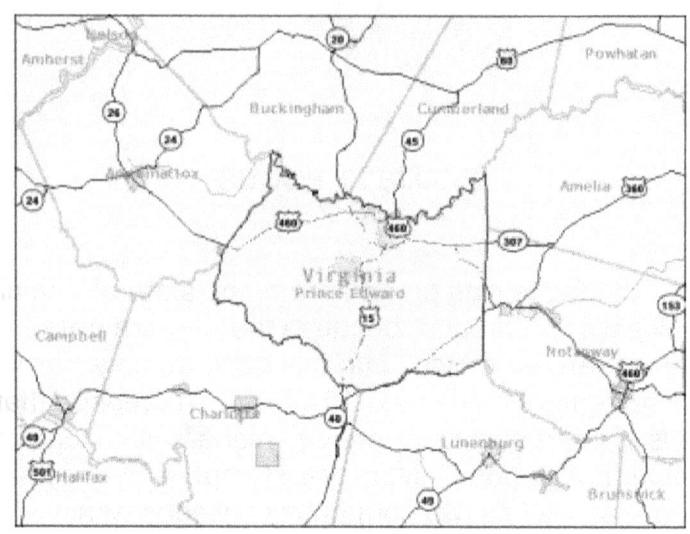

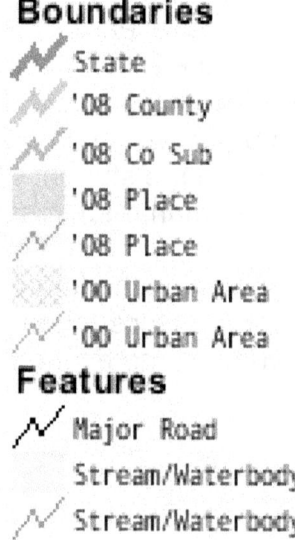

Figure 1. Map of Prince Edward County, Virginia – Location: SouthWest of Richmond, Virginia

Looking at the growth of the area in employees available for that economic area, there would be an increasing need for support and services from government and private entities such as educational schools, municipal support (hospitals, highways, garbage collection, local government support services) (BLS, 2010).

The census indicated a rise of approximately 19,000 new workers (or available employees) in the Farmville area over the last 10 years (approximately 2,000 annually). To accommodate the influx of new citizens in the area, there would also need to be housing (construction and renovation), retail establishments serving the growing population (groceries, restaurants, drug stores, hospital medical providers), as well as a growing police force to service the locality.

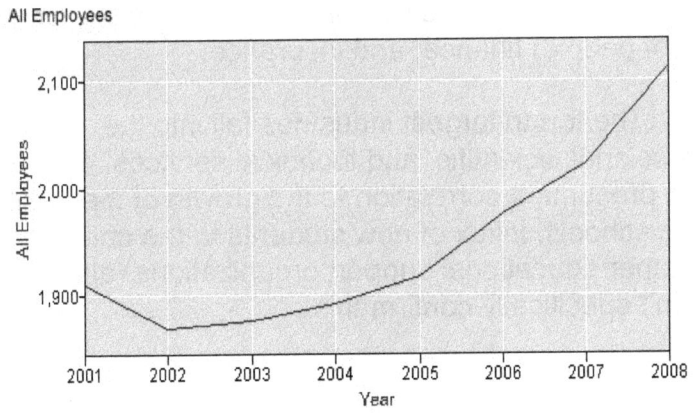

Figure 2. All Available Employees in Prince Edward County Virginia; Education and Health Services; All Establishment Sizes

Table 1. *Statistical Growth of Available Employees in Prince Edward County Virginia; Education and Health Services; All Establishment Sizes*

Year	Jan	Feb	Mar	Apr	May	Jun	Jul	Aug	Sep	Oct	Nov	Dec	Annual
2001	1921	1905	1902	1906	1930	1913	1902	1911	1923	1901	1900	1904	1910
2002	1840	1866	1870	1863	1857	1900	1903	1920	1901	1836	1819	1861	1870
2003	1865	1861	1873	1875	1875	1949	1918	1930	1929	1821	1815	1814	1877
2004	1877	1865	1883	1879	1914	1935	1884	1917	1920	1874	1881	1877	1892
2005	1863	1882	1904	1913	1960	1947	1907	1935	1952	1927	1917	1902	1917
2006	1879	1898	1920	1969	1989	2052	1952	1990	1994	2035	2029	2001	1976
2007	1998	2026	2009	2046	2081	2016	1978	2004	2010	2057	2037	2016	2023
2008	2055	2070	2033	2093	2098	2121	2107	2150	2135	2171	2163	2168	2114
2009	2169(P)	2168(P)	2224(P)	2214(P)	2191(P)	2190(P)	2207(P)	2229(P)	2260(P)				

P : Preliminary.

The following table indicates the current state of the economy and the various types of economic based industries located in Prince Edward county (VA), of which there are ~500 noted with the number of employees (by size of company). The US census bureau had identified the types of businesses in this geographic area, whereas the most prevalent are retail trade, followed by construction, then (interesting for the ratio of people) finance, and insurance.

The fourth largest industries fall into the professional, scientific, and technical services, and one could presume a correlation to the growth of the local public schools, influx of new students to the colleges, and other educational support organizations (albeit data doesn't specifically confirm this).

Table 2. *County Business Patterns (CBP), Metro Business Patterns (MBP), and Zip Code Business Patterns (ZBP) in Prince Edward County Virginia*

Industry Code	# of Establishments by Employment-size class & Industry Code Description	Total Estab.	4-Jan	9-May	19-Oct	# of EE's 20-49	# of EE's 50-99	# of EE's 100-249	# of EE's 250-499
------	Total	499	235	124	65	54	10	8	3
11----	Forestry, fishing, hunting, and agricultural	2	1	1	0	0	0	0	0
22----	Utilities	1	0	0	0	1	0	0	0
23----	Construction	61	41	14	4	1	1	0	0
31----	Manufacturing	13	5	0	3	3	1	1	0
42----	Wholesale trade	22	10	6	3	3	0	0	0
44----	Retail trade	112	51	26	17	13	2	2	1
48----	Transportation & warehousing	5	3	2	0	0	0	0	0
51----	Information	9	2	2	3	2	0	0	0
52----	Finance & insurance	33	15	12	4	2	0	0	0
53----	Real estate & rental & leasing	18	13	4	1	0	0	0	0
54----	Prof., scientific & tech. services	28	20	6	2	0	0	0	0
55----	Management of co's. & enterprises	2	0	1	0	1	0	0	0
56----	Admin, support, waste mgt, remediation services	7	4	0	1	1	1	0	0

Industry Code	# of Establishments by Employment-size class & Industry Code Description	Total Estab.	4-Jan	9-May	19-Oct	# of EE's 20-49	# of EE's 50-99	# of EE's 100-249	# of EE's 250-499
61----	Educational services	3	1	1	0	0	0	1	0
62----	Health care and social assistance	77	23	25	13	8	2	4	2
71----	Arts, entertainment & recreation	7	2	2	1	2	0	0	0
72----	Accommodation & food services	47	14	7	8	15	3	0	0
81----	Other services (except public administration	52	30	15	5	2	0	0	0

The number of schools seem relatively low for the geographic area. It could be conceivable to forecast the number of elementary and secondary schools in the area would have a need to either increase in size or have additional schools built (or add portable classrooms) to accommodate the increasing number of youth in the growing population. There were ~6,600 children of school ages (between 'under 5 years of age' and 19) in the US census bureau's database in 2008. With three primary and secondary educational schools, the population growth may foretell over-crowding in those three schools.

Prince Edward Public Schools provided education to 2,770 pre-kindergarten to 12th grade students from Farmville and throughout the 357-square-mile county, in 10 buildings servicing the elementary school, a middle school, and a high school. The elementary school provided educational services to grades pre-K through grade four in a campus-style facility. The middle school serviced grades five through eight. The high school offered over 20 dual enrollment courses, ranging from calculus to electronics.

The Career and Technical Education (CTE) Center offered classes in business, information technology, computer-assisted drafting (CAD), auto servicing, electronics, health/medical sciences, family/consumer sciences, construction and building trades, and agriculture/horticulture programs. Additionally, the high school supported a two-way, audio-video instructional classroom.

Dual enrollment classes coordinated with Longwood University, as well as Hampton-Sydney College. Prince Edward schools employed 450 personnel, of which about 260 were faculty and administration. It was noted approximately 41% of the faculty had graduate degrees. Nearby Cumberland County public schools had a population of circa 1,400 students, and coordinated with nearby Southside Virginia Community College for dual-enrollment students (Farmville Area Chamber of Commerce, 2010).

Table 3. *Educational Services in Prince Edward County, Virginia, 2010*

Industry Code	Industry Code Description	Total Estabs.	4-Jan	9-May	19-Oct	# of EE's 20-49	# of EE's 50-99	# of EE's 100-249	# of EE's 250-499
61----	Educational services	3	1	1	0	0	0	1	0
611110	Elementary & secondary schools	1	0	0	0	0	0	1	0
611610	Fine arts schools	1	0	1	0	0	0	0	0
611710	Educational support services	1	1	0	0	0	0	0	0

Table 4. *Demographics - Sex & Age in Prince Edward County, Virginia – 2008 (Total School Age = 6,600)*

SEX AND AGE ACS Demographic and Housing Estimates	Estimate	Margin of Error	Percent	Margin of Error
Total population	21,455	*****	21,455	(X)
Male	10,818	+/-238	50.4%	+/-1.1
Female	10,637	+/-238	49.6%	+/-1.1
Under 5 years	1,018	*****	4.7%	*****
5 to 9 years	1,159	+/-268	5.4%	+/-1.2
10 to 14 years	1,107	+/-291	5.2%	+/-1.4
15 to 19 years	3,316	+/-885	15.5%	+/-4.1
20 to 24 years	3,167	+/-735	14.8%	+/-3.4
25 to 34 years	1,898	+/-523	8.8%	+/-2.4
35 to 44 years	2,588	+/-438	12.1%	+/-2.0
45 to 54 years	2,338	+/-303	10.9%	+/-1.4

SEX AND AGE				
ACS Demographic and Housing Estimates	Estimate	Margin of Error	Percent	Margin of Error
55 to 59 years	844	+/-230	3.9%	+/-1.1
60 to 64 years	1,054	+/-230	4.9%	+/-1.1
65 to 74 years	1,485	+/-170	6.9%	+/-0.8
75 to 84 years	1,046	+/-198	4.9%	+/-0.9
85 years and over	435	+/-184	2.0%	+/-0.9
Median age (years)	30.3	+/-0.3	(X)	(X)
18 years and over	17,573	*****	81.9%	*****
21 years and over	14,138	+/-864	65.9%	+/-4.0
62 years and over	3,645	+/-207	17.0%	+/-1.0
65 years and over	2,966	*****	13.8%	****

Longwood University was home to between 4,300-4,500 students, and Hampton-Sydney College provided education to an additional 1,000 students. At the time of this research project, Southwest Community College provided two-year degree classes and certification programs for about 8,000 students. Combined, the local primary, secondary, and advanced education institutions in this geographic area serviced ~20,000 students which was almost equivalent to the number of citizens living in the county of Prince Edward.

In addition to the local (physical) schools, there are four Higher Education Centers that partner with schools across the state to bring course curriculum to students who are unable to attend campus classes via satellite technology. The Higher Education Institute in Martinsville, VA partnered with 11 different universities in the state of Virginia. The Roanoke-Higher Education Center partnered with 12 other colleges and universities in the state of Virginia. The Southern Virginia Higher Education Center partnered with eight colleges and two foundations (certification programs). The Southwest Virginia Higher Education Center (SVHEC) partnered with eight colleges and universities.

What does this mean for workforce development in this region? The researcher's forecast was if the population increased as the past 10 year trends, land prices will rise in conjunction with the demand for housing. This action will be coupled with the need for more construction, building, and service industries. Local government support services (infrastructure) will be in higher demand, as the taxable base (personal property, sales taxes, other local revenue sources) from which the local governments pay for the rising cost of that infrastructure.

There will be a growing need for the local population's educators and instructors at the primary and secondary level, but also college and university professors and adjunct faculty at the nearby institutions of higher learning. A higher demand from the higher education centers may cause the local colleges and universities to be compelled to provide more educational opportunities and training courses, specifically related to those currently being farmed off to other colleges and universities across the state, to try to retain those 'dollars' for tuition to be funneled back into the local county economy and tax-based institutions of learning.

Another possibility is ... many retiring baby boomers may consider getting away from the higher population cities in Virginia (Roanoke, Washington, DC., Richmond, southeastern Virginia) to an even more rural 'retirement' community still large enough to support a hospital (emergency medical health care facilities), or even consider moving north from the North Carolina area of Raleigh, Greensboro, or Durham, if the cost of living is relatively low.

A demographic study for Amelia, Buckingham, Charlotte, Cumberland, Lunenburg, and Prince Edward counties noted 43% of the area's employed residents (or about 15,600 individuals) commute to jobs outside the area, according to a Wadley-Donovan Group (WDG) survey. This might be because the economy cannot support the trade skills or knowledge skills of those living in the area, or there is not a large enough manufacturing or trade industry in the immediate area to support those 'employable' within the available workforce.

> "Retail skills constitute the single largest category with 20%, followed by manufacturing maintenance, manufacturing other than highly skilled, and agriculture-related occupations, each with 13% of non-employed residents. The manufacturing skills as reported by non-employed residents are precisely those skills that are currently, and projected to be, in demand by local employers (CRC, 2010)."

An interesting note on the CRC site stated close to 50% of the area's residents have an interest in receiving training to acquire new skills for career development. This translates to just under 19,000 individuals. The skill sets in which they have the highest interests are: computer science agriculture, fishing, mining, medical, and education related services. This could be a huge potential for the local educational institutions to target potential learners to provide these educational services (although not necessarily a guarantee those services would be marketable in the immediate years after graduation from the program in the local area).

To summarize the information noted above, it seems there is a huge potential for basic and continuing educational services in this identified area of the state of Virginia. Those with the capability to teach or train in the areas of highest interest to the local citizens, as well as those who could provide training instruction to learners of those institutions of higher learning, could potentially find a 'calling' there. There does need to be a more concerted effort for the local Chamber of Commerce, Better Business Bureau, Regional Workforce Development, Commonwealth Regional Council, and other business organizations to entice more, and more large-scale, businesses to the area to support the future workforce once they have learned the new skills (if they do get that opportunity).

For businesses, the relatively-lower wages for that part of the state (cost of living, etc.) should entice potential new county citizens to move or start businesses into the area, where companies would have a large workforce from which to pick the best and the brightest for their staffing needs with a lower cost and/or overhead. If the workforce could be trained on many of the cognitive skills marketed as telecommuting work, there may be an opportunity for businesses to use those skilled workers still in the United States versus farming the work out to foreign countries.

Information obtained from the Chamber of Commerce and Visitor's Bureau coupled with information from the Workforce Training & Development research assignment, could provide feasible and practical recommendations for improving workforce readiness and capability in this strategic plan. The focus area is Prince Edward County / Farmville, VA. This plan, in partnership with local businesses, the mayor and town manager, the seven-member city council, and local business and institutional representatives, should positively impact the per capita income for the local citizens and workforce population.

Information was retrieved from the U.S. Census, Bureau of Labor Statistics, Farmville Area Business Directory, the Farmville Area Chamber of Commerce, Commonwealth Regional Council, and a 2010 Virginia Employment Commission Community Profile. Key data used to develop this strategic plan noted:

- Prince Edward County has circa 21,200 citizens, the City of Farmville ~7,000, and nearby Cumberland County at about 9,000 (VEC, 2010; Farmville Area Business Directory, 2010; Farmville Chamber of Commerce, 2009; U.S. Census, 2000)
- Median annual family income in the city of Farmville is $33K ($13,552 per capita) and Prince Edward County is $48K (Farmville Area Chamber of Commerce, 2009)
- 50% of the area's residents are 'interested in obtaining new skills for career development,' which equates to ~10,600 citizens (CRC, 2010), which reflects a potential geo-centric correlation for a need for new skills training/adaption against a 2009 9.3-10% unemployment rate (VEC, 2010).
- 40% have 'some high school' to associate's degree-level of education (VEC, 2010)
- The highest population group of age-ranges are between 19 to 24 years old, with the second and third highest groups being 39 to 49 and 10 to 14 years of

age respectively (VEC, 2010)
- Predominant business type for the top 20 employers are: Education (4), Food and Retail (7), Health (4), Government (3), Job Development (1), and Manufacturing (1) (VEC, 2010)
- Largest non-government occupations in the area are: 1) food preparation (53%), 2) production/manufacturing (26%), and construction/extraction (23%) (VEC, 2010)
- Projected new hire needs (industry) are, in order: Accommodations/Food Industry (highest turnover), followed by Healthcare/Social Assistance, Educational Services, and Retail Services (VEC, 2010).
- A Crossroads Services Board can assist with placement, career training, transportation, work adjustment training, job coach training services, transitional employment, individual- and group-support
- The city of Farmville is a historically charming, but modern small city, economically focused on tourism, education, hospital/health services, and manufacturing (furniture) (Boyer, 2010)[1]

The following objectives were tendered to: 1) improve the economy and tax revenue, 2) increase overall workforce capabilities, and 3) serve business profitability in the geo-area for hiring and retention. The strategies and initiatives based upon human cooperation and scheduling availabilities, so a tentative timeline was projected in general terms only.

---

[1] *Personal trip to Farmville and Price Edward County, July 4th, 2010, included visits to the campus of Longwood University, Hampden-Sydney College, the Farmville's Visitor Center, and the town of Meherrin.*

Goal I – Research and Coordinate – availability of educational/training resources and identify potential future sources and funding to increase training/education workforce development capabilities. The long-term goal is to attract businesses researching new/added locations in the south-central area of Virginia because of a highly capable, trained workforce – with little employer-based (overhead) training needed to ensure a retail- or wholesale-unit, or a manufacturing division is profitable within a timely-period.

Strategies / Objectives	Outcomes / Measures	Projected Timeline
1. Inventory available local, regional, public, and private training sources with the viewpoint of becoming stakeholder partners in the future economic and workforce development of the geo-area 2. Encourage local businesses and large employers to provide space, funds, cooperative efforts in staffing, representatives to the workforce effort, and coordination with local government officials to train current employees, but	• Documentation of available sources for education and training in a one-stop document for reference and referral by potential learners • Free resources prioritized and verified • Low cost resources identified / documented • Find business training-partners in industry that would enable a more technically proficient workforce by seeking direct training funding from large businesses via outreach opportunities • Grant funding sought by committee effort, individuals, and/or business entities to	Between six to 12 months to research, document, report, and market to local business entities and public/private sector POC's; another six to nine months to put training in place after development, locations ID'ed, funded, and staffed

Strategies / Objectives	Outcomes / Measures	Projected Timeline
also potential future employees 3. Map educational locations and capabilities to avoid overlap in educational and/or training availability 4. Strive towards providing technology capabilities training (Internet, email, basic office software, etc.); research IT tech companies' training and educational grants / funding 5. Research TARP and other grants (private, public, government [Fed/State] for funding; as well as solicit local business initiatives 6. Target the highest number of population age group(s) to provide more ROI on workforce training directives	enrich program / expand offerings to more • Outcome – document identifying available (with any cost) resources for career and skills training in local geographic area	

A review of outcomes and measurements used to ensure the strategies and objectives were being reached and occurred monthly, with a review committee involving local city officials, representatives of the larger local employers, as well as representatives of the local public and private school systems and organizations. It is important these multiple representatives partake of this effort to increase accomplishments aligned with the local geographic area and region, and could be intertwined with government funding and grants for programs within their own institutions, which could potentially increase if the scope is broader and more encompassing.

Goal II – Combine, Fund, and Provide Resources - to provide more ROI (or avoid duplication of funding for multiple training venues) to increase the number of city/county citizens who have access to and availability to the training and education via private sector, joint coordination of efforts between local secondary schools and higher education centers, and partnering with local private entities, churches, non-profits, and organizations to increase available workforce development training for venues and number of programs.

Strategies / Objectives	Outcomes / Measures	Projected Timeline
1. Survey businesses (as stakeholder partners) for alignment of vital training needs – baseline skills, soft employment and career skills, or specific/unique (hard) work-related skill sets, career, or professional knowledge or aptitudes	• List of most desired, general workforce skills attributable to the highest turnover job 'types' towards which workforce training can be directed to reduce 'costs' of replacement • Improve the entry-level, employability	Once training needs established; with a target goal of 5-10% of the 'employable' workforce trained annually within approximately 12 months;

Strategies / Objectives	Outcomes / Measures	Projected Timeline
2. Create training modules covering inter-related learning (ex: baseline math and writing skills, ESL, entry level career skills, soft employment skills, register operations and customer service skills) 3. Assign 'buckets' of vital training needs for public and private sector into groups with locations that are most relevant to the population needing the training and the availability of resources, equipment, and/or facilitators of the training/education 4. Increase the number of available training modules for the general public and workforce 5. Advertise the availability of the training initiatives via word of mouth, social groups, social media (Internet), local business announcements, media (business flyers and newspapers), and career counseling offices, as well as at	of the highest number of county/city residents in the geo-area • Increased awareness of local workforce of available training and education • Reduce employer base-line training, which increases profit margins through reduction of training costs • Retain more in-area workforce (vs. commuting out of area) to increase per capita tax sources to local government and for a more robust local business recruiting pool • Increase the numbers of capable employees within the geo-area • The largest number of age groups get additional and vital training for workforce capability (KSA's) • Outcome: Turnover reduction in local businesses, increased retention / tenure of entry-level employees,	

Strategies / Objectives	Outcomes / Measures	Projected Timeline
the VEC, college campus and high school guidance offices, etc.	increase in-area employee opportunities, decrease in commuting workforce outside the geo-area	

A review of outcomes/measurements used to ensure objectives were reached should provide proof via increasing time of tenure for employees, a reduction of commuters leaving the county/city for outside work, and increased profit margins for businesses operations resulting in an increased tax revenue stream for the city and state. As 'word gets around' to social groups, more will take advantage of the training and education program offerings. Evidence of workforce training development working would be indicative by five new or small businesses or at least one mid-size or large business opening or moving into the geo-area based on workforce capability/availability every 2-3 years.

Goal III – Market and Promote – The local Farmville (city) and Prince Edward County tax base is constrained by the low per capita income for the geographic location, so it is in their best interests to promote the area for: 1) increased tourism, 2) rich numbers of locality-based educational institutions, and 3) opportunities to provide trained and ready workforce workers for new business and market entities for physical workforce needs, but also telecommuting-able workers.

Strategies / Objectives	Outcomes / Measures	Projected Timeline
1. Chamber of Commerce and Business Development representatives continue outreach to entice new employers and businesses (and start-ups) within the local geo-area using increasingly trained workforce	• Increase number of businesses in the local geo-area, which in turn, provides a higher stream of tax revenue • Increase in number of workforce training opportunities, with increase in funding from tax revenue, and potential increase in partnership, stakeholder funding of training opportunities • Outcome: increased numbers of workers, potential decrease of commuting workers outside the county/city resulting in increased payroll and other tax-based (sales) income	This is a long-term project timeline over the course of a five to ten-year period, as well as an ongoing goal past the ten-year period

A review of the outcomes and measurements used to ensure objectives were being reached should provide documentation of new and planned businesses in the geo-area, as well as increased growth of population above the current rate of 11.32% projected between now and 2020.

Co-Worker Partnership w/ Local Employers

The researcher and spouse owned a carpet cleaning company, Monster Clean,[2] in the Hampton Roads geographic Tidewater area in Virginia which was growing exponentially with a high demand for domestic cleaning, commercial properties, and government facilities. Based on the interviews conducted on another assignment in this class noting the absence of soft skills for the entry-level workforce, the researcher focused on cooperative training between the company and outreach organizations in this geographic area.

Employees come onboard 'fresh' with no training in carpet or upholstery cleaning. Most employees have high-school diplomas. Monster Clean had two full-time employees and two part-time employees. A new truck would allow the company to hire another 2-3 employees.[3] The company had also received an award for a GSA schedule, and would be concentrating efforts in contract sales to the federal, state, and local governments. In the future, some of the company's full-time workers would be assigned supervisory duties and would need further soft- and hard-skill training in paperwork, payroll, and scheduling as the company expanded, hired more workers, and purchased more trucks.

It will be hard to define what cooperative efforts can be established between local organizations and the Monster Clean's current workforce and training needs to be provided for Monster Clean. There was a need for

---

[2] www.MonsterClean.com
[3] *Monster Clean was currently losing between $400-$500 daily due to inability to accommodate the customer demand with only one truck. A new truck delivery (expected last week of July of 2010) to accommodate current / future demand.*

carpet cleaning technology training for all levels (and ages) of the Monster Clean workforce. The company advertised all carpet-cleaning teams had a trained technician supervising the work completed for each job. Monster Clean relied on a local janitorial supplier (Cleaner's Closet) that brought in external 'specialists' to provide accredited International Institute of Cleaning and Restoration Certification (IICRC) training to learners.

  The next step for Monster Clean was to strive towards opening a rug cleaning plant.[4] This means the company would need to hire and train supervisors and drivers to run the equipment, as well as pick up and deliver rugs for customers. The Better Business Bureau, the Retail Alliance, and the local Chamber of Commerce would be networking partners in marketing the company, as well as putting out the word about hiring needs. Career One Stop, Nex-Step, and the Virginia Employment Commission was a good source to work with for different aspects of the company's need to develop the company workforce. Monster Clean could partner with these organizations to obtain potential sources of future full-time employees and to provide job training (temporary internships) for those interested in learning more about carpet and upholstery cleaning for career opportunities. If potential employees had gone through soft-skill programs within those organizations, they would have a higher probability of being hired by Monster Clean.

  Career One-Stop did not have any training programs directly related to carpet cleaning or janitorial services, but they did have training programs related to customer service and drivers. Nex-Step was more a job posting service, similar to the Virginia Employment

---

[4] There was only one in the Hampton Roads geographic area as of summer of 2010.

Commission, which assists in training via The Job Training Partnership Act, which helped to:

> ...establish programs to prepare youth and adults facing serious barriers to employment for participation in the labor force by providing job training and other services that will result in increased employment and earnings, increased educational and occupational skills, and decreased welfare dependency, thereby improving the quality of the work force and enhancing the productivity and competitiveness of the Nation (The Job Training Partnership Act, 1982).

The Virginia Beach courts have a cooperative association with the National Guard Youth ChalleNGe Program© at Camp Pendleton which takes 'troubled youth' to reshape their attitudes, and train them physically, which Monster Clean could have targeted for potential workers. Monster Clean was also be open to hiring rehabilitated felons. These two employee sources would need soft- and hard-skills training; soft via the local organizations and hard skills via on-the-job training and in-class technical training, as they accomplished the minimum number of months with the company.

The biggest potential issue for hiring employees for this company was the work was tedious and boring, workers are exposed to heat (hot steam lines in summer and winter) and extreme cold (during winter months), and they must be physically capable of lifting heavy equipment, including going up and down stairs with the equipment. The incentive was the workers get paid commission, but did not have to sell, although they could increase individual commission (take-home pay) by up-selling additional cleaning services or products. The employees had to be capable of performing math 'on the spot' to ensure the customer got charged correctly as well as computing the correct commission for payroll. These academic skills were necessary, as well as customer service skills in communicating to the customers are vital for the business.

The owner also needed further training. To get up to speed on accounting and bookkeeping principals for QuickBooks software, he had to take advantage of the local education system for software training provided by the city of Virginia Beach (Adult Education Center next to the Central Library on Virginia Beach Boulevard).

This plan would increase the ROI for company training, and pool resources for lower training overhead costs, while preparing or offering a cheaper venue for basic job skills training. Simultaneously the company would be gaining access to newly trained potential job candidates. Monster Clean did recognize the value of community-based training and education organizations.

The area in which the researcher focused for large workforce employers in the Hampton Roads, VA area, in the seven-city area of Virginia Beach, Norfolk, Portsmouth, Suffolk, Chesapeake, Hampton (including Yorktown), and Newport News. The researcher focused on internal T&D provided to employees (EE's) either internally designed or provided externally via vendors. (Responses are sentence fragments to reduce length of overall paper.) The POC's, with the identifying acronyms used to ID each response to the questions are noted below:

Research survey interviewees were anonymized in this book but the companies with whom they were employed were identified to document validity of the researcher's sources.

1. (DT) (anonymous) Director of Field Training and Development, Dollar Tree Stores, Inc., HQ's, 500 Volvo Parkway, Chesapeake, VA   http://www.dollartree.com

2. (WC) (anonymous) SPHR, WorkersChoiceUSA, 5700 Cleveland St., Va. Beach, www.workerschoiceusa.com

3. (NAVY) (anonymous) PHR, MSFSC/N161, 471 East C Street, Norfolk, VA; Website: www.msc.navy.mil/civmar/training.htm

4. (CMA) (anonymous) Mgr., T&D, CMA CGM LLC, 5701 Lake Wright Dr., Norfolk, VA; www.cma-cgm.com

Note: Where there was no response noted below for each question, the answer was NA or None.

Key to acronyms:

EE = Employee
RVP = Regional Vice President
CSR = Customer Service Representative
T&D = Training & Development
WOTC = Work Opportunity Tax Credit
OJT = On the Job Training

Questions with Interview Answers

1. **How do you conduct an internal 'needs assessment' for your workforce?**

(DT) - Find the root-cause for the training needs, gaps, deltas, and then use Bloom's taxonomy for program/content design; soon to deploy an LMS and e-learning in the future based on assessments for learning from bottom-up; hands-on, cognitive-based training, OJT, in-field training for store associates, managers, and district managers. As organization has grown/matured, so have leaders.

(WC) - Skills based assessments, reviewing the six most important skills/knowledge needed to perform the tasks based on job. There are six training quizzes for new EEs to ensure not memorized information, but they are able to find the info to answer customer questions. Includes: 1) underwriting, 2) collections, 3) verifying income, 4) verifying employment, 5) anti-money laundering laws, and 6) various loan products based on Federal/State lending laws; 'open book,' testing; required within 30 days of hire; training hidden agenda = increase EE's self-confidence.

(NAVY) – Needs assessment is related to special ratings & credentialing required on ship(s).

(CMA) - We interview managers for needs; compile a report for executives, discuss how it ties to org. & strategic goals for the company, determine priorities, as well as prior requests. This workforce assessment is conducted annually as a team effort. Management workshops in place for core competencies for individual's transitioning to leadership. The newest challenge is growing and implementing a leadership program.

2. **Do you / how do you conduct an external 'needs assessment' for future workforce?**

(DT) - Determine how to recruit higher-caliber EEs for management levels (near-future goal).

(WC) – None per se. Surprisingly, most EEs hired have acceptable math skills for job tasks; while writing skills seem to lag below standards. Some mentoring occurs within for writing skills for peers and co-workers. Some EEs are sent to seminars for work-related skills (math/Excel) or business writing.

(CMA) - The Process Engineering Department is implementing a CSR problem resolution databank to enhance and speed up the problem resolution. Currently the CSR's are creative in solving concerns, so they may not be eager to find they are now required to use a 'standardized' methodology for resolving future issues. Hopefully, once trained, they will see the benefits.

3. **Do you conduct an analysis of needs and build a training program around the needs, or does the company have an established set of criteria historically used for training within the ranks?**

(DT) - Historically, training was standardized repetition of skill sets. Now, there is a need's based, 'targeted to specific person, store, district' needs based training conducted.

(WC) - At Corporate HQ's, lawyers & lobbyists keep HR/COO abreast of new laws, federal and state lending changes and mandates for industry, notifies HQ's, then changes are reviewed, discussed, and if vital, incorporated into training quizzes, as well as instruct Regional Vice Presidents of changes. The company uses historic training in place (example: Truth in Lending Act). Try to foresee future lending laws and issues which may affect the business overall, as well as down to the training needs for each store.

(NAVY) - Helped develop training programs; mostly needs related to career pathing.

(CMA) - New hires – on-boarding, support, mentoring (buddy system), workshops for soft skills, technical proficiency, interpersonal, leadership program (cross-training), and for overall company, customer problem resolution is the primary focus of training within the company (USA).

4. **Do you primarily concentrate on specific skills training such as software, manufacturing, sales methods, and processes or is T&D focused more on general organizational skills (leadership, management, organization behavior)?**

(DT) - As the more formalized and specific training was put in place, specific metrics have been attached, ROI has improved; training leadership has improved; training for district managers - 'lynch-point.'

(WC) - Concentrate on training related to finance; specific to storefronts. There have been two 'soft skill' training events in last three years. Because of the geographic location of RVP's across the country, it is more advantageous to complete one-on-one training via teleconference to focus on personal skills training, with the T&D Manager.

(NAVY) - Focus more on specialized technical skills, including engineering, applied sciences such as culinary arts for chefs, deck training for officers and other service members on ships.

(CMA) - The company provided tuition reimbursement for 100% of tuition up to $4K annually for courses with an A/B grade. Program is so successful; it had to be capped at a ceiling of $55K.

5. **Do you have any external programs associated with workforce development in the local geographic areas to develop future EEs of the company?**

(CMA) - There is a cooperative program with the ODU Maritime program.

6. **Do you find you need to provide remedial training for any of your EEs related to basic educational skills and knowledge such as reading or math?**

(WC) - Fortunately, most hires do reasonably well with the simple math skills required to service customers; and simple calculations such as calculating monthly income from a per hour salary.

(NAVY) - Provide some remedial training for those who have difficulty passing tests for credentialing and licensing; some courses are difficult enough there are a few failures.

(CMA) - No. There are performance tests and a resource lab for EEs which offers in-house training for management, business knowledge, organizational effectiveness, career development, and professional growth; computer application training available via an external vendor; in addition to tuition reimbursement.

7. **If yes, how to you accommodate those training needs?**

(WC) - Past three years, training to improve current skills, such as Excel; business writing.

(NAVY) - Those needing remediation, matched up with a mentor who already had the training.

8. **Do you measure any ROI on company's efforts to train EEs within those programs?**

(DT) - ROI is hard to prove specifically with this type of training. The best metric to address with this is retention/turnover. Metrics are available; hard to prove training result.

(NAVY) - Measure those #'s of completed credentialing & licensing, those who are undergoing the training.

(CMA) - ROI is not as important as ensuring the training is available and provided to the EEs as needed. There is an

impact, which can be measured against business changes, and behavior changes ROI might be a little too hard to prove compared to the business impact.

9. **What training program is the most prevalent within the company – which level of EE is it directed toward?**

(DT) - District Managers (DM) –focus more on district leadership skills; Dollar Tree wants to focus on coaching and developing future leaders for the company. Teach, learn, and teach.

(WC) - Skills based training, specific to the storefront level with six training modules.

(NAVY) - Upwards career path training programs are the most prevalent.

(CMA) - Training is directed: 1) Import/Export Training, 2. Business Process Engineering, 3. New hire orientation/on-boarding, and 4. Leadership Development Program – focusing on coaching, initiative, etc.

10. **Does the nature of your business (foci) require you recruit new hires for general business jobs, industrially specific business, or (working on) government facilities?**

(WC) - General business recruiting focuses on storefront associates (lowest level). Since industry has a fast 'burn-out' rate, the RVP will call HQ to call for new associates, job posted, then RVP's does hiring.

(NAVY) - The general focus is to identify where there are deficiencies & need for career path certifications, licensures, etc., that would assist the military service member in achieving the next rank.

(CMA) - This business is so specialized, tends to focus on hiring those with specialized and unique skills.

11. What seems to be the most difficult piece of finding qualified candidates to work for your company – 1) general knowledge and education, 2) "soft" capability and skills, or 3) "hard" unique skills sets, knowledge, and understanding of industry or specific tasks to be performed?

(DT) - More complex; economic, legal, HR issues - opportunities to become more knowledgeable at field level with all of the above, and drive training.

(WC) - The most difficult to find are the 'soft skills' - good business ethics, shows for work on time and dresses appropriately. The hiring process includes a telephone interview and face-to-face interview, and scoring capability (by hiring manager). Many RVP's hire more for personality and 'fit' than scores. RVP's prefer to look for candidate's ability to smile, get along, and perform positive customer service practices.

(NAVY) - There does need to be some pre-requisite courses for technical training required for leadership.

(CMA) – It is difficult to fill billets with qualified people for jobs mostly of a tech nature (logistics, import/export, warehousing) - revolve around computer technology - must be capable of learning.

12. Do you have a process to determine the Return on Investment (ROI) for the training that is performed within the business?

(DT) - Stores move between 1-5 million pieces (each store, annually), so that will have an impact from appropriate training and ROI measures.

(NAVY) - We collect data; provide reports to management.

(CMA) - There are personality type tests (MAP) which assists in supporting ROI, but don't drive decisions.

13. Is the training referred to in annual performance evaluations and part of the annual review requirements and/or compensation considerations?

(DT) - Training specifically is not evaluated at levels. Indirectly, we address it. This is a future opportunity.

(WC) - EEs with company over 30 days are provided what are called "annual celebrations" of work performance. Emphasis is on positive feedback, constructive criticism, and discussion of future performance to increase value to company, how to make next year's "annual celebration" even better.

(NAVY) - This training can be part of the annual performance evaluations, but are concentrated more on career pathing and advancement training; so they may be suggested or advised during the evaluation.

(CMA) - Not as much as they should; trying to plan training in conjunction with the annual performance evaluations, but currently underutilized; potential for an improvement arena, but not a driver.

14. Are managers, supervisors, and executives responsible for the achievement or use of training of their subordinates throughout the training, in annual budgeting for training needs, as well as reporting summary evaluations of training outcomes?

(WC) - The supervisors are held accountable for achievement of initial six-module training for new hires. New hires have incentive to complete training within first 30 days for additional fifty cents per hour salary.

(NAVY) - The training department has a tracking system for deficiency reports; these are used in coordination with supervisor and/or advisors to assist in planning of the training, who, when, where, etc.

(CMA) - There is no charge-back for the training, and managers of departments are not tasked to include training in their budgets.

If any training is needed, they are required to put in a request, and document the need based on job tasks and skills currently in place, then the training department will assist.

15. If you don't have an established workforce development program within your company; what would you like to see put into place to establish this program?

(WC) - A T&D program within the company held on a quarterly basis for all the RVP's in each district - optimum, in addition to bi-annual with RVP's in a group setting. T&D Manager solicits ideas, feedback, review company's recent activity for best-practice solutions & discussions during these training events.

(CMA) - Would like approval for a massive sales training initiative to positively affect profits. Executives are supportive, but T&D department can't provide everything within budget. (Increase ceiling for tuition reimbursement, for example.)

16. How would the program help the company reach its strategic objectives and/or goals; and what is holding the company back?

(WC) - Company strategy is to grow portfolio of loans, and assist customers in feeling good about coming to the company for loans, as well as paying them back. Staff don't communicate with other storefronts in the same district. District staff should meet one day each quarter to discuss ideas/communicate; like to provide more training to district and store managers in business development, marketing, and public relations to the locality, businesses near the company's storefronts, and people in the community.

(NAVY) - The training is required for safety, mission, regulatory mandates to avoid injury, and to save ships and their crew during their mission for national defense.

(CMA) - The biggest holdback is time and ability to get everything done.

17. Does your company obtain or seek any federal, state, or local grants to assist you in workforce training?

(DT) - Work Opportunity Tax Credit (WOTC) for certain individuals – hiring and training.

(WC) - In Louisiana, the company takes advantage of specific federal tax incentives to hire EEs in hard-hit economic areas resulting from hurricane Katrina (possibly WOTC?).

(CMA) – Initially chose Norfolk for HQ's for state/local grants for workforce development.

18. Are there any national or state standards required for any of your workforce (jobs specifically) for your industry?

(DT) - OSHA, food handling since started food sales and annual/bi-annual sexual harassment.

(WC) - Formal evaluations - not in place; informal evaluations - when EE completes six-modules.

(NAVY) - Some standardized annual training (personal information privacy), sexual harassment, safety specific to ships, some specialty training such as high voltage safety for ships.

19. How do you evaluate your training? 1) Formative or 2) summative?

(DT) - Summative evaluations mostly; some formative throughout the training, but mostly looking for behavioral changes via observation evaluations, as well as impact on metrics.

(NAVY) - The department uses several vendors; most use tests to evaluate the trainees for pass/fail; the vendors provide feedback, but they don't come back later to evaluate the trainees in a formal venue. Supervisors may observe behavior later for learning, but nothing formalized.

(CMA) - Level 1 Evaluations – within each workshop. Level 2 Evaluations – observation, classroom, some pre- and post-testing, mostly for skills development. Best practice - perform one-on-one interviews with learners after the training, but time-prohibitive.

20. **Does training provide certifications or assist the EEs in obtaining external (to company) certifications, recognized by the company, industry, or other companies?**

(DT) - Yes – depending upon the disciplines; for example the HR department encourages PHR, SPHR certification in the HQ's / corporate locations; but not so much out in the field.

(WC) - Certificates were issued in past for completion of the training; but indicators were EEs didn't place much value on the certificates. Can't significantly monitor training, so certs. of no value as a validation tool.

(NAVY) - This training department doesn't do certificates for completed training, but data is entered into a skill database. Vendors might offer specialized certifications - IT related learning (LAN Admin, A+, etc.).

(CMA) - Some regulatory training required due to the nature of business – OSHA, Hazard Training, safety, etc. Some Subject Matter Experts certified to teach whom issue 'certificates' to learners completing classes. The company provides 'pretty certificates' for those training courses available online.

21. **How to you plan for workforce replacement due to 'baby boomers' retiring or executive replacement as the vital or key EEs start leaving the company?**

(DT) - Leadership T&D programs ins place; uses case studies, field experience, and works with managers for content when developing & writing training programs. Scenario building is used for live responses, pre-testing, and post-testing used for

development of thinking (cognitive) skills building.

(WC) - This industry is a 'burn-out' profession; many EEs rarely last past two - three years. The HQ's offices (administration) are static; no one there is ready to retire. Company discovered 'maturity' of \ new hire will reflect type of skills training. 'Older' workers = computer technology; 'younger' workers = business ethics (time, attendance, as well as communications).

(NAVY) - Some individuals get forecasts for promotional positions, and start training for requirements for billet; training requirements are determined to schedule training for learners in a future track, job pathing.

(CMA) - The foci the last two to three years on succession is mostly within the executive team and department heads; those are one-on-one development/mentoring. Career progression with development of EEs for future career mapping, career pathing - concentrating on sales, management, and customer care.

22. How often are your T&D programs revised or updated, and what factors cause those to be reviewed for updating?

(DT) - At least quarterly, updating and revising T&D programs – in part, to ensure evergreen with any procedural changes and continue to evolve development programs.

(WC) - Ideally every 12 months the six new hire training manuals need revision for new regulations and laws based on state or federal legislation. Three years ago, all stores were provided with three-ring binders, printed and mailed from HQ's. Now conducted via an electronic web-based training package.

(NAVY) - Mostly provided by vendors; must meet Coast Guard credentialing requirements and standards, and are evaluated every five years.

(CMA) - No SOP for updating; unofficially training reviewed by managers; then objectives identified; modules adjusted for elements, target group(s), content, pre-requisites, length, materials, and processes. There are three leadership programs in review, including: Interview processes and behavioral styles; mandatory/direct reports for legal aspects, law changes; and management streamlining of processes, and emotional intelligence.

Summary of Interviews

Results of interviews showed companies conducted some needs assessments, but none seem more than minimally involved in external training to local work-force. Training was standardized, specific to in-house jobs and skills needed, and changes occur only for legislation or as needed by management. The soft skills versus specific or technical skills provisions resulted in a 50/50 split for skills training and level of employee, and remedial training seems to be minimal.

Only one company worked with external organizations for local workforce development and most used WOTC where feasible. ROI was only conducted as a numbers report, and felt it was too hard and time consuming to analyze metrics. While training was part of annual performance evaluations there was little ROI or 'connecting the dots' analysis performed. Internal certificates of training completion are worth only the value of the paper on which they are printed. Succession planning may be in place, and executives focus on cognitive skills.

Proposed Program:

This is hard to define as a need for cooperative efforts between most companies and the workforce that is available, and what definitive training really needs to be provided in-between secondary school and the workforce available. From these interviews, there seems to be a need for technology training for all levels and ages of the workforce, and apparently either the high schools are not providing skills to be 'employable' or not enough training on those to learners to be competitive after graduation for local jobs.

This researcher would propose the Better Business Bureau, the Retail Alliance, and the local Chamber of Commerce (as a collaborative effort) team with local community colleges and local employers (via those businesses with memberships to the organizations) to provide training on basic employment skills to the local workforce market. This program could be applied to more than one locality, but across the US in all cities and counties (localities), do develop the workforce, with potential employers being provided the ability to access 'employable' job candidates simultaneously.

There may additionally be some government grants, which could be focused on funding a portion of the overhead costs to schools and trainers. Other job training programs might also be encouraged to participate, including One Stop, Nex-Step, state unemployment commissions. Program training packages sold to the companies who are members of the organization would be able to support some of the trainer salaries, as well as purchase (or lease space) for use of equipment in the computer labs.

It should not be free to the workforce (folks will value something more if they must pay to get it). The researcher would suggest a nominal or monthly fee ($20) to join a Job Skills Enhancement 'club.' Companies can sponsor entry-level employees to attend for the same fee (paid directly by the employer), which would be more cost effective and have more ROI than internal training.

The training would be held at local community colleges or high schools (nights / weekends), provide formal classes for 30 minutes to learn a new tech skill, and allow for lab practice (based on problems set in real-life work situations to emphasize practical benefits). Or the employer could pay for a set-aside class for a group of employees for training for a unique skill. Most who need this training would appreciate the 'short' sessions to be in bite-sized learning.

This plan would increase the ROI for company

training, and pool resources for lowered training overhead costs, while preparing or offering a less expensive venue for basic job skills training, while simultaneously gaining access to those newly trained potential job candidates.

It seems many of the companies are not interested in ROI from the evaluation viewpoint, but do recognize its value, and simply may not have the time or incentive to apply or analyze the outcomes other than basic numbers reporting. Part of the proposed program's 'value added' might be to offer a ROI as a report to employers for funneling 'up the food chain' to prove value, as well as the employer's ability to participate in job-placement programs for those completing the base-line training for math and business writing skills.

RETURN ON INVESTMENT PLAN

This return on investment plan (ROI) will highlight the company in which the researcher was partnered with their spouse. Monster Clean's goal was to grow the carpet-cleaning business to keep two truck-mounted cleaning plants running 5-7 days a week and to eventually have enough profitability to open a rug cleaning facility in Hampton Roads. The company had been in business for 10 years, and in the last four years (2006-2010) had experienced exponential growth. More than 2,500 domestic customers (repeat and referral business), and over 150 commercial clients (including GSA schedule federal government customers) regularly purchased Monster Clean's services. The business objective was to convert every customer into a 'Monster Clean evangelist,' so the customers referred the company in positive conversations to future clients. The company made enough of a profit margin to comfortably operate the business, but – the company always put the customer first – no matter the cost (or profit loss!). Customers recognized Monster Clean's reputation as stellar and unsurpassed.

The primary mission of the business was to give the customer a perceived 'more than they paid for' value in services. The Hedgehog Concept (Collins, 2005) recognized our investment values as: 1) passion, 2) best at, and 3) the resource engine. The owner's passion for the business and what they did for their customers was obvious. One of the owners may be described as obnoxious (loud, booming voice). After listening to him talk about his 'monster' truck and the carpet cleaning capability, the listener would understand and recognize his pride in ownership and excitement about the business and his passion about a commitment to doing 110% for his customers. Monster Clean's risk-reversal policy relieves new customers' anxiety. If the customer is not happy with our performance in the first room, the company would pack up the equipment, say "sorry for the trouble," leave, without the customer owing a dime. Monster Clean had *never* been fired.

The company owners recognized customers have a psychological need to be assured they will get their carpets cleaned, and when the company service providers were done, the customers often reflected the carpets look new or almost like-new. The company owner's passion and confidence had a positive ROI when the customers become regular, repeat clients. Because the customers are happy with the company's services, they advertised for the company … for free. When the company's service reps spent an extra few minutes talking to the customers, getting to know them, explaining exactly what is going to be done to their carpets – as if they were family – then the customers couldn't wait to tell their neighbors, friends, family, and co-workers about the results.

This effort to personalize the business had allowed Monster Clean to drop a $30K full-page annual yellow pages advertisement - one of the most astounding ROI's this company had realized. Over the last two years (2008-2010), Monster Clean had been able to use a much smaller percentage of the savings of $60K (two years of yellow-book advertising costs) toward a more concentrated and targeted marketing efforts, further increasing Monster Clean's return on investment for advertising dollars.

In the last three years (2007-2010), Monster Clean had recognized merely talking about the company, or having the customer talk about us, didn't make the company a recognized expert in the business. The company strived toward social recognition in the form of awards as part of their branding. At the end of 2007, Monster Clean encouraged customers to submit positive reports to reporting agencies such as Angie's List, and more recently, to Google, Yahoo, and other Internet based entities.

If a customer was unhappy with any work Monster Clean had performed, the owner goes back and works on the issue until the customer was satisfied. Efforts to please the customers and pro-active branding resulted in two Carpet and Upholstery Vendor of the Year awards for Hampton Roads from Angie's List for 2008 and 2009 (requirements are hearty and strict), and the company was on line for winning, again, in 2010. Additionally, Monster Clean was able to win "Best of" awards in 2010 for Norfolk, Portsmouth, Chesapeake, Suffolk, and Virginia Beach (silver and gold), with advertising placed only in Virginia Beach (the other cities were won by write-ins).

The social marketing ROI for these marketing efforts provided surprising results. When the economy took a downturn in late 2009, some of the company's competitors pulled out of the business or had a serious drop of income,[5] while Monster Clean realized an increase in business because customers decided to clean versus replace their carpets.

---

[5] Which for some continues today (as of 2010), according to a local janitorial supplier for these local businesses.

Monster Clean's resource engine is technology knowledge, equipment that is unique to the entire state of Virginia, personal desire to do the best for our customers, and the recent award of a GSA schedule to perform work for federal, state, and local government(s). The company was willing to work seven days a week, up to 12-hours daily, providing customers' services per their schedules. The company had injected money into getting the best equipment (truck-mounted, diesel-engine powered, steam), had invested money in training of workers (IIRCC certifications in three levels [basic, intermediate, and advanced] of carpet & upholstery cleaning, moisture remediation, and odor remediation), and spending the man-power and vehicle expenses to provide personal quotes, if desired, for domestic customers, as well as commercial clients.

The company's branding was ongoing, constant, and a daily achievement of social science. The owner/partners attend business network meetings sponsored by the Chamber of Commerce and Retail Alliance in 'belly-to-belly' events. The owner/partners also presented to groups, attended business network groups, and sponsored one of their own (Business Brainstorming & Network Exchange, 2010).

Future efforts to provide additional ROI for business strategic goals were as follows.

ROI events –

The strategic plan of the company was to get as many employees trained and certified in IIRCC certifications of carpet care (moisture remediation, odor remediation, special care and cleaning, etc.) to ensure our advertising promise of a trained technician on every job. When Monster Clean scheduled a crew, one of two employees in the truck has certified training. If the owner was forced to work in the truck, he was unable to devote time to marketing and providing quotes, thus sales slowed down.

Reaction –

The employees were prepared and eager to attend the classes and obtain the certification. Monster Clean waited until employees are on the job for approximately six months before investing in the training course. The courses ran from one to two days, depending upon the certification, and the cost was between $250 and $550.

Learning –

Training was provided to employees via an in-class course, which also included testing for summative evaluation. The employees were paid an hourly wage while in the course, as well as the company covered the cost of the course. The total out of company pocket cost could run $330 to $630 per employee.

Application –

The quality cleaning and knowledge of the technicians of the company was part of the vital component of the company's advertising. For contract jobs, where there may be some question about the methodology of the cleaning for unique spots, carpet composition, or remediation, the owner would visit the job site to confirm the technician(s) treated the carpets correctly. The technicians carried certification cards with them (similar to credit cards, with the completed classes/certifications listed) to every job.

Business Impact –

The impact of business was that when the owner must jump back into the truck to work, there was a reduced value of his time and capability to get out to market the company to obtain new customers or repeat business from past clients. This was impacted by pushing jobs into the future, which reduced the same day or weekly income, as well as pushing back immediate revenue from new contract business that same day.

Data Analysis –

The cost of carpet cleaning was dependent upon the number of rooms cleaned, the number of domestic homes cleaned each day, whether the job is domestic or commercial. Gross revenues for 2009 was $160K, calculated to a five day, eight-hour, workweek makes the revenue (gross) average to about $76.92 per hour.[6] The

---

[6] *These figures do not take into consideration overhead, equipment, and business operating costs – they only value the total gross receipts compared to the number of hours of an average worker at 40 hours per week, five days a week, 52 weeks per year.*

employees averaged about $15.00 per hour (although they actually earn 15% commission on each pre-sold sales ticket versus working for an hourly wage), resulting in the owner's value at about $61.92 per hour, $2,476.80 a week, or $128,793.60 annually.[7] What could not be measured was the value of contracts or jobs postponed into the future when the crews couldn't get to the location or for down-time. The cost of sending an employee to a technical certification class ran between $330 to $630 per employee, plus $495.36 to $990.72 (for the owner's time), for a total of about $825.36 to $1,620.72 for 1-2 days of training. The cost of one day training could be recouped in one day of domestic carpet cleaning jobs, two-days of training are equivalent to about two days of carpet cleaning revenue.

The total impact of training for the Monster Clean workforce was simple. Each training class completed by employees could be recouped in 1-2 days of revenue stream, while the savings were also equivalent to approximately 1-2 days of owner's cost of time saved by not having to pull the owner off his marketing and sales tasks to work the jobs not being worked by his technicians. The goal of the company was to not only have six employees on staff by this time next year (2011), but also to have no less than three employees with at least two certifications 'in their pocket.' Costs would be equivalent to ~$4,952 over the course of the next year (2011), recouped within approximately five to seven days of work.

---

[7] This figured does not take into consideration 'replacement' of the $15.00 per hour employee not on a current job – but you can multiply $15 times eight hours to deduct $120 per day the owner is subbing for employee(s) in class.

References

Boyer, D. (2010) *Workforce training needs of the Prince William County and Farmville, VA area.* Unpublished manuscript.
Bureau of Labor Statistics. (2010). Retrieved from: www.bls.gov.
Business Brainstorming & Network Exchange. (2010). Retrieved from http://www.meetup.com/BizBrain-Network
Career One-Stop. (n.d.). Retrieved from www.careeronestop.org/TRAINING/TrainingEduHome.asp
Carnevale, A. P. and Desrochers, D. M. (2003). *Standards for What? The economic roots of K-16 reform.* Retrieved from: www.transitionmathproject.org/resources/doc/topicindex/standards_for_what.pdf
Clagett, M. G. (2006). *Workforce development in the United States: An overview.* Download from: skillscommission.org/pdf/Staff%20Papers/ACII_WIA_Summary.pdf
Collins, J. (2005). *Good to Great and the Social Sectors: A Monograph to Accompany Good to Great.* ISBN: 0977326403
Commonwealth Regional Council (CRC). (2010). Retrieved from: http://www.virginiasheartland.org/demographics.html
Farmville Area Chamber of Commerce (2009). Farmville Area Chamber of Commerce - Virginia (Prince Edward County, Farmville, and Cumberland County). In Chamber of Commerce (Ed.), (pp. 1-69). Farmville, VA: The Village Profile.
Farmville Area Chamber of Commerce. (2010). Retrieved from: http://www.farmvilleareachamber.org
Friedman, T. (2005). *It's a flat world, after all.* The New York Times, April 3, 2005. Download from: www.nytimes.com/2005/04/03/magazine/03DOMINANCE.html?ei=5070&en=8a8 a8c4c3a6ca791&ex=1178337600&pagewanted=print&position=
Hampton-Sydney College, College Rd, Hampden-Sydney, VA 23943. (2010) Retrieved from www.hsc.edu
Higher Education Institutes, New College Institute, Martinsville, Virginia. (2010). Retrieved from: www.newcollegeinstitute.org/
Longwood University, 201 High St, Farmville, VA. (2010), Retrieved from: www.longwood.edu
Mangum Economic Consulting, LLC. (2008). *The role of workforce-related noncredit education and training in Virginia's Economy.* Download from: myfuture.vccs.edu/Portals/0/ContentAreas/Workforce/NoncreditAnalysis071008.pdf
National Center on Education and the Economy. (2008). *Tough choices or tough times: The report of the new commission on the skills of the American workforce.* (Revised Edition). San Francisco, CA: Jossey-Bass. ISBN: 0470267569
National Guard Youth ChalleNGe Program©. (n.d.). Retrieved from www.ngycp.org/site/node/13
Nex-Step Organization, (n.d.). Retrieved from www.nex-step.org/

Phillips, J. J. (2003). *Return on investment in training and performance improvement programs* (2nd Ed.). Burlington, MA: Butterworth-Heinemann Publications. ISBN: 0-7506-7601-9

Roanoke Higher Education Center, Roanoke, Virginia. (2010). Retrieved from: www.education.edu/

Southern Virginia Higher Education Center, South Boston, VA. (2010). Retrieved from: www.svheducation.org/index.html

Southside Virginia Community College, 1041 W 10th St., Blackstone, VA 23824. (2010). Retrieved from www.sv.vccs.edu

Southwest Virginia Higher Education Center Abingdon, VA. (2010). Retrieved from: www.swcenter.edu/

The Job Training Partnership Act, (Pub.L. 97-300, 29 U.S.C. § 1501, et seq.) C.F.R. (1982, 1992, 1994).

The State Council of Higher Education for Virginia (SCHEV). (2010). Retrieved from: www.schev.edu/students/collegeListAlpha.asp

The United States Census Bureau. (2010). Retrieved from: factfinder.census.gov/servlet/ADPTable?_bm=y&-geo_id=05000US51147&-qr_name=ACS_2008_3YR_G00_DP3YR5&-context=adp&-ds_name=&-tree_id=3308&-_lang=en&-redoLog=false&-format=

The United States Census Bureau. (2010). Retrieved from: www.census.gov/econ/cbp/index.html

The Virginia Employment Commission. (2010). Retrieved from www.alex.vec.virginia.gov/lmi/pdfs/communityprofiles/5104000147.pdf

Wagner, A. (2006). *Measuring up internationally: Developing skills and knowledge for the global knowledge economy*. Download from: www.highereducation.org/reports/muint/MUP06-International.pdf

ABOUT THE AUTHOR

Dawn D. Boyer, Ph.D. completed her Doctor of Philosophy in Education (Occupational & Technical Studies, with a concentration in Training & Development in Human Resources) from Old Dominion University in Norfolk, VA in 2013. Her dissertation is entitled, 'Competencies of Human Resources Practitioners within the Government Contracting Industry,' which identified unique KSAs for Human Resources Managers working for federal level government contracting companies. This groundbreaking research is the impetus upon her recently released textbook guide for Human Resources Professionals in Government Contracting, available on Amazon.

She has been an entrepreneur and business owner for 14+ years, currently in her consulting firm, D. Boyer Consulting, based in Richmond (Henrico County), VA, and servicing clients internationally. Her background experience is 24+ years in the Human Resources field, of which 11 years are within the federal defense contracting industry.

Dr. Boyer's experience in federal (defense) contracting as a Human Resources Director or Senior Manager provided her a subject matter expert insight, experience, practice, and capabilities to perform within this industry, as well as the ability to instruct others to KSAs needed in middle-management or executive human resource roles.

Dr. Boyer works with job and new career seekers to write Search Engine Optimized resumes for increased visibility to recruiters – getting the candidates past the recruiting 'firewall' and interviewed for faster hires and job placement. Her tech-based knowledge of how the ATS software systems work help job seekers in structuring a resume for recruiters' Boolean search queries. Her SEO coding within resume is so unique, no other resume writers offer this service.

She assists academics and writers publish their works or manuscripts as a third-party publisher – DBC Publishing. She also assists business owners in developoing their brand and marketing plans within social media marketing, planning, and management.

She is the author of over 155 books on the topics of genealogy, family lineage, academic education, human resources and government contracting, women and gender studies, business, and career search practice, quotes for self-improvement and motivation (2,000+ /3,000+ series), and her 'Interview with an Artist' series (three artists in the series to date). All her books are listed on her Amazon author's page at:

https://www.amazon.com/author/dawnboyer.

Dr. Boyer has been a member of LinkedIn since 2004 (a few months after beta version released) and has developed a rich profile for consistent and constant communications to ~12,600+ connections. Her clients call her 'The Queen of LinkedIn.'

She may be reached via her business website:

http://DBoyerConsulting.com
or by email:
Dawn.Boyer@DBoyerConsulting.com

CURRICULUM VITAE

DAWN D. BOYER, Ph.D.

B.F.A., M.Ad.Ed., CDR, CIR, LSS - Green Belt

- 24+ years, HR, Employee Relations, Recruiting, Training, Development, Presentations, Benefits/Compensation, Analysis/Auditing, and Employment Law/ Practices
- 15+ years, Entrepreneur, Business Owner, Business Partner
- 11+ years, Federal Defense Contractors (SBA 8(a), HUB Zone, Service Disabled Veteran Owned Business, Woman Owned, and Alaskan Native Corporation [ANC])
- 11+ years, Federal / Government Contracts Employment Issues and Laws
- 8+ years, Teaching, Training and Curriculum Development in business, information technology, and Human Resources in proprietary and public educational institutions
- 7+ years, Contracts, Negotiations, and Insurance Benefits Administration
- 3+ years, Graduate Teaching Assistant (GTA) for Undergraduate Studies

EMPLOYMENT HISTORY

08/10 - present, Resume Writing Subject Matter Expert, Social Media Management Consultant, Editing & Publishing (dba DBC Publishing), D. Boyer Consulting, Virginia Beach and Richmond, VA

12/15 – 06/16, Adjunct Professor, Art Institute of Virginia Beach, VA

06/15 – 2016, Reviewer/Editor, Academic Publications

08/09 – 12/12, Adjunct Instructor & Doctoral Graduate Teaching Assistant, Old Dominion University, Norfolk, VA

06/07 – 09/17, Vice President / HR Director, Business Development, and Social Media Manager
Monster Clean, Carpet, Oriental Rug & Upholstery Cleaning, Virginia Beach, VA

11/07 – 03/09, Director
Human Resources & Ethics Compliance
Chenega Advanced Solutions & Engineering, LLC, Norfolk, VA

05/05 – 11/07, Senior Corporate Recruiting Manager, Zel Technologies, LLC (ZelTech), Hampton, VA

01/03 – 04/05, Human Resources Manager (Corporate Specialist), AMSEC LLC (Corp HQ's) (a LLC between SAIC & Northrop Grumman Newport News Shipbuilding), Virginia Beach, VA (Corporate HQ's), (Subsidiary companies: Egan McAllister & Associates (EMA), PMI, M. Rosenblatt & Son, Inc., etc.)

03/01 – 01/03, AMSEC Human Resources Manager, LLC (IMEG / SETS Group)

07/95 – 01/01, Human Resources Manager, Norfolk Warehouse Mgmt. / The Taylor Cos., Norfolk, VA

12/94 - 07/95, Human Resources Creative Generalist, Metro Information Services, Inc., Va. Beach, VA

FORMAL EDUCATION

Doctor of Philosophy (PhD), **Old Dominion University**, Norfolk, VA; *Occupational and Technical Studies (Science, Technology, Engineering & Math in Professional Studies (STEMPS); concentration in Training & Development in Human Resources; GPA: 3.65*

Masters Degree in Education, Virginia Commonwealth University, Richmond, VA (1989), Adult Education - Human Resources, Training & Development, Personnel, and Staffing; GPA: 3.67

Bachelors Degree in Fine Art, Advertising, and Graphic Illustration, Radford University, Radford, VA (1983); Graphic Advertising & Illustration, Fine Art, and Art History; GPA: 3.25

Follow the Author on Social Media Platforms

D. Boyer Consulting
DBoyerConsulting.com

Join her 12,600+ connections on LinkedIn:
www.linkedin.com/in/DawnBoyer

Amazon Author Page:
www.amazon.com/author/dawnboyer

Review Author's books:
www.shelfari.com/DawnDeniseBoyer

Twitter at:
www.Twitter.com/Dawn_Boyer

YouTube Channel:
www.youtube.com/user/DawnDeniseBoyer

Interested in publishing your own
academic essays, projects, or books?
Contact the author for publishing project estimates,
consulting, and assistance:

Dawn.Boyer@me.com

www.DBoyerConsulting.com

ABOUT THE BOOK

Between 2009 and 2012 the author completed coursework for a Doctorate of Philosophy in Occupational and Technical Studies (STEMPS), with a concentration on Training and Development in Human Resources. The Ph.D. coursework and research was conducted and completed at Old Dominion University, Norfolk, VA.

One of the mandatory program courses was Trends and Issues of Economics and Workforce Development and was completed in the Fall of 2010. The course required completion of several segments of research, analysis, interviews, surveys, and application of findings to a report that provided suggested curriculum development and workforce training based on the findings and literature reviews.

This book provides the student's examples of coursework completed per the mandated project work, and conclusions based on the research and analysis work during this class. The book can be used as a model guideline to completing similar project in this class for future students, or as a baseline model upon which to complete workforce development research focused within a specific geographic area.